Old Kilmarnock's Shops
Frank Beattie

John Greenway established a glass and china shop in Kilmarnock in 1870. In 1882 the shop was in Portland Street and John was living in John Finnie Street. By 1900 John was in Dundonald Road and the business, retail and wholesale, was run by John Greenway and James Cook as Greenway and Cook.

© Frank Beattie, 2022
First published in the United Kingdom, 2022,
by Stenlake Publishing Ltd.
54-58 Mill Square,
Catrine, KA5 6RD

www.stenlake.co.uk

ISBN 978-1-84033-931-4

The publishers regret that they cannot supply copies of any pictures featured in this book.

Printed by
P2D Books, 1 Newlands Rd,
Westoning, Bedford, MK45 5LD

Acknowledgements

Fraser Beattie, John Donaldson, Kevin Donaldson, Alan Marsh, Frank Spence, Ian Faulds and John Gall

When asking older folk about their favourite shops in Kilmarnock, one name that kept coming up was the oddly named, Utilitarium. This shop had its roots in 1844. It later had an Ayr branch and the firm lasted into the second half of the 20th century, when the Kilmarnock branch was in Market Lane. It sold just about everything. When the Utilitarium closed the distinctive building, seen here, was taken over by Lewis's, a department store that had adjacent property and a main frontage facing on to King Street.

Introduction

Shopping is something we all do. A long time ago, before there were many shops, people would spend five days a week making and preparing their products, usually at home. Then one day a week they would go to the market and set up a stall to sell their products. Sunday, of course, was a day of rest.

Various dates between 1609 and 1612 are given by different historians for a visit to Kilmarnock by Timothy Pont. His visit is important because he left a good description of the town as it was when he saw it. He said Kilmarnock was a large village in great repair and that there was a weekly market. This, presumably, was for all goods.

About 1705 the town's Meal Market was built in High Street. For many years this was the only place in Kilmarnock where meal could be sold to the people of the town.

A sheep and cattle market was established in Kilmarnock in 1789. It was held each Tuesday. Kilmarnock became a great cheese centre and in the middle of the 19th century the butter market was in the Agricultural Hall, now the Grand Hall.

Gradually, many traders moved into their own properties. These were the first shops. Some successful businesses ended up with more than one shop, either in the town or in the district. Some shops were large and sold nearly everything. They used grand names like the Emporium or the Utilitarium.

Shopping changed greatly in the early 20th century with the arrival of national chains.

F W Woolworth opened a 3d and 6d shop at the corner of King Street and Market Lane in Kilmarnock in 1925. Marks and Spencer opened a new branch of their business in King Street, Kilmarnock, in September, 1936. Boots the Chemists was well established as a national chain when they opened in King Street, Kilmarnock in 1937.

Even in the 1960s, most of the shops in the core shopping area were locally owned. The trend towards national and international chains continued, but there was an even bigger change coming; the rise of the supermarkets.

The 1957 Kilmarnock trades directory lists 81 grocery shops. At that time, many housewives went shopping every day, sometimes more than once a day, because they were restricted to what they could carry, the corner grocer's shop was a short walk from home, and it was a place to catch up with the gossip of the street.

Some innovative grocery shops started using the system of providing a basket and letting customers pick their items off the shelves.

Kilmarnock's first large, custom-built supermarket was Fine Fare which opened in August, 1970 at the corner of Titchfield Street and West Netherton Street. It went through various name changes, closed in 2004 and was demolished in 2007. Today the site is another supermarket, Aldi.

Supermarkets also changed, extending the range of goods offered from groceries to everything and providing customer toilets and sometimes a café.

Today supermarkets dominate the sale of goods from shops, but now, they too are under threat from the latest change to shopping. Technology allows anyone to sit at home with a computer, or just a phone access any trader and order and pay for whatever they want without leaving home. Where will shopping be in the future?

John Boyle was a drysalter. His business was established in 1874 and he dealt with wholesale and retail. He was at 123 King Street, in a building next door to the old King Street Church. John Ferguson had a grocery shop at 121 King Street and specifically advertised teas and whiskies.

The food rationing scheme was designed to ensure that everyone wartime and post-war in the country got a fair share of wholesome and healthy food. The diet was devised by nutritionist, John Boyd Orr, 1880-1971, who came from Kilmaurs and attended Kilmarnock Academy. After the war he became the director general of the United Nations Food and Agricultural Organisation and was awarded the Nobel Peace prize in 1949.

R.B.1 13 — 1

MINISTRY OF FOOD

RATION BOOK

(GENERAL) 1950-1951

Surname Henry

Initials — NATIONAL REGISTRATION NUMBER

Address 36, WAVERLEY AVENUE
(as on Identity Card)
KILMARNOCK, AYRSHIRE
(For change of address)

FOOD OFFICE CODE No. WS17 — Serial No. of Ration Book BC 260706

IF FOUND RETURN TO ANY FOOD OFFICE

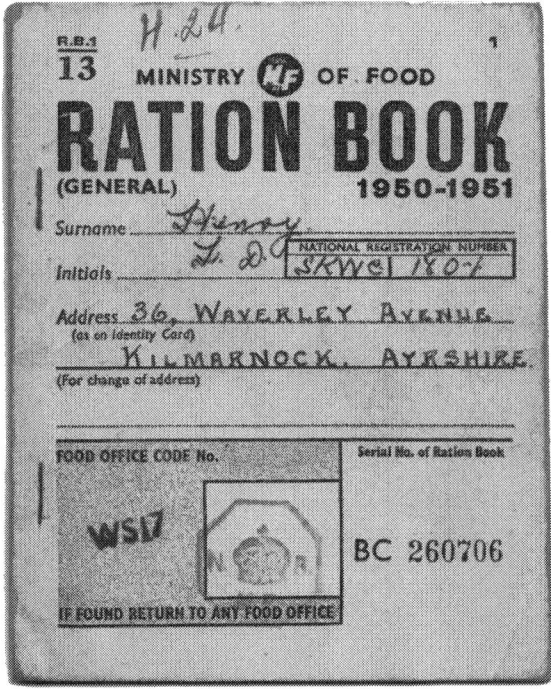

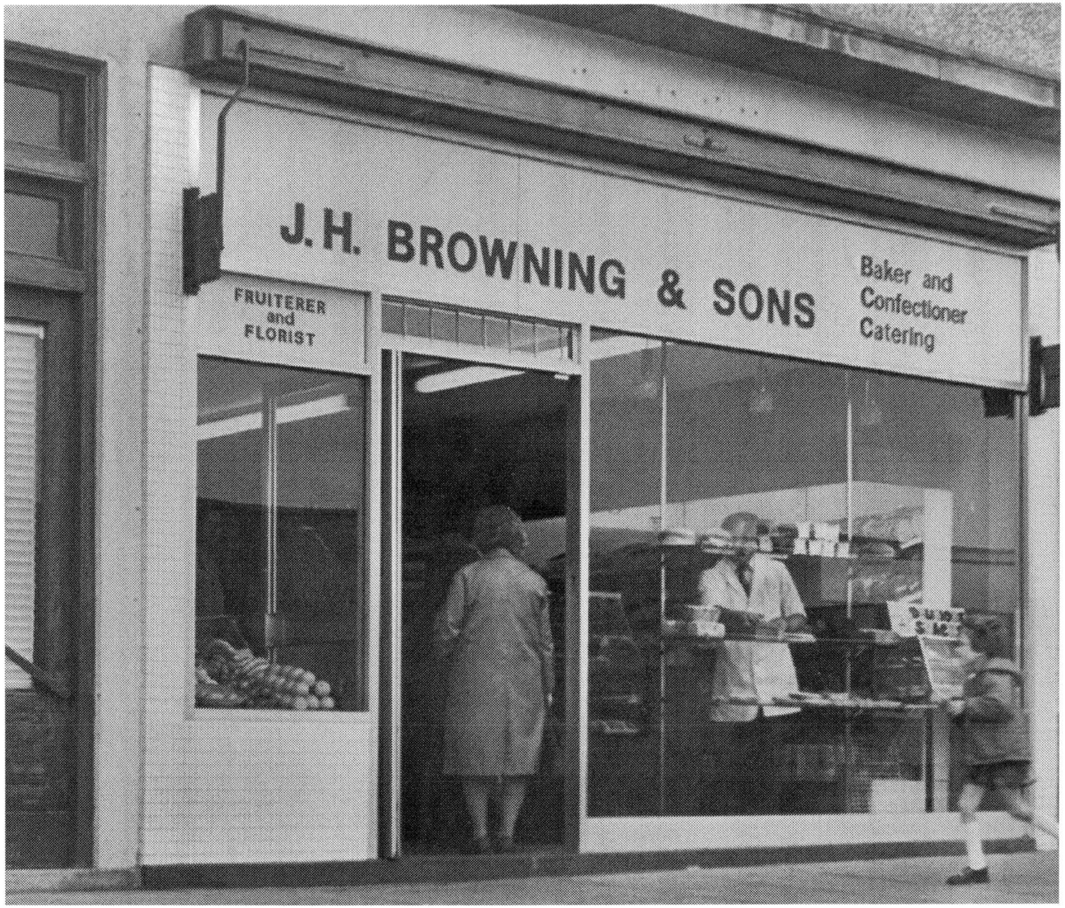

As peace returned to the world, the local family business of Browning the baker was established in Kilmarnock in 1945 by Jack Browning. The business continues to thrive. In 2003 the firm was named British Baker of the Year in the Baking Industry Awards in London. Today they have their own chain of shops and supply supermarkets with selected products. Note that in this old picture, they were also florists and fruiterers. It was Jack (John) Howie Browning who started the business, hence the original company name of JH Browning and Sons. Today the business is in the hands of John Gall, son of the daughter of Jack Browning. John Gall has shown that local businesses can transform themselves into major players in the national market.

William Cairns was a fishmomger, based in Cheapside Street in the 1970s. The 1957 Directory lists him at 29 Old Street, Riccarton. The same family had a cafe in Waterloo Street. The Cairns Tea Room and Elsie Milne (Née Cairns) did most of the baking.

Shopping began to change in the 1960s, though it wasn't quite recognised at the time what a big impact the new supermarkets and multi-nationals would eventually have. TF Campbell was a typical local shop. It was not just a record shop. They also sold toys, prams, bicycles and just about anything that the proprietor fancied selling. In 1960 T F Campbell was taken over by Ayrshire Wireless Services Ltd, but it continued to trade under the name of T F Campbell. Time caught up with the business, which closed its shop in King Street about 50 years ago.

Clarks Umbrella shop was in King Street and it is seen here all dressed up for the Coronation in 1953. In the 1890 street directory, David Clark is listed as an umbrella maker at 12 Green Street and as a draper and clothier at 7 Portland Street. In 1904 he had, additionally a shop at 8 King Street.

picture from Jean Nairn

Kilmarnock had a tram system from 1904 to 1926. In this picture the tram makes its way up Portland Street towards the railway station. The photograph is from about 1906 and was taken when Portland Street was a busy shopping area.

Inspired (belatedly) by the pioneering work of the Fenwick Weavers Society, which founded the world's first co-op in 1769, a group of people in Kilmarnock formed their own co-operative society in 1866. The Kilmarnock Equitable Co-op Society grew rapidly and soon had branches in all parts of the town. This one was in Portland Street. The last quarter of the 20th century saw great changes in the town centre and Portland Street began to be cleared for new developments. This Co-op building was demolished in 1990. Sandstone figures from the façade, representing industry, were retained and placed in the car park across the road from the site of the original building.

John Dorkin ran a short lived tailoring business in Portland Street in the early 1920s.

The drapery business of G A McMurray seems to have been established in Kilmarnock in the 1880s. Early trading was from two shops, one at the Cross and one at West George Street. The company later moved into Portland Street, where they had a large department store. With changes in shopping habits, the large shop was closed and a smaller one concentrating on fashion was opened in King Street about 1980. Three generations of the family have run the business. Unfortunately the fashion shop opened by the new generation of the McMurray family did not survive the harsh economic circumstances and the business was closed.

In 1890 Alex Weir started a boot and shoe shop in Portland Street. The business grew into a major drapery and clothing shop, which traded as Weir's of Portland Street, until its final closure in 2000.

David Faulds opened a family butcher shop business in High Glencairn Street, Kilmarnock in 1896. Now, four generations later, the business is run by David's great grandson, Ian, who keeps to traditional methods and local sources. He cuts meat from carcasses. Unlike previous generations when these were hung in the shop and attracted all sorts of flies (or even outside the shop in Stewart's advertisement *above*), today's carcasses are kept in a closed chilled area on the premises. He has a loyal customer base and is known for quality service. Unfortunately, most of the company history has been lost and it seems that, at one time, the documents and photos relating to the company history were simply disposed of.

William Paterson

Established 1835.
Telephone No. 308.

FAMILY BUTCHER,
SAUSAGE MANUFACTURER :: AND POULTERER. ::

Sausages a Speciality, made Fresh daily.
Black and White Puddings.

ORDERS CALLED FOR AND DELIVERED
:: EVERY MORNING WHEN DESIRED. ::

.: Corned Beef and Pickled Tongues. ::
Finest Quality Home-Fed Beef and Mutton.

16-18, Duke St., Kilmarnock

The family-owned butcher shop business, McGarrity, was established in Kilmarnock in 1950. They were in Waterloo Street and Stevenson Street near the corner with Yorke Place. Later on the business was in the Foregate.

In 2017 Flowers by Karen in Bank Street took over the neighbouring shop that had been used by Watson's hairdresser to expand their business. In 2019 the two shops were reshaped into one shop.

This local florist and fruit shop opened in 1873 and was in business for more than 130 years. The shop closed in 2005. The last owner was Bryan McLaughlan, the third generation to run the business.

Ferri's ice cream was first sold in Kilmarnock in 1923. Michael Ferri, senior, had a base in College Wynd and sold his ice cream from his bicycle. In 1941 Ferri's moved into property on the corner of Titchfield Street and Armour Street and it is still there today. As well as ice cream, Ferri's is popular for fish and chips.

picture from the Kilmarnock Standard

The Forum Cafe was established in 1937 to serve customers of the Forum Cinema in Titchfield Street. After the closure of the cinema the cafe, known and advertised as Pieroni's continued and gained a high reputation for the quality of their ice cream. With redevelopment of the Titchfield Street site, the Forum moved to High Glencairn Street into property previously used by the Royal Cafe. Today, the business is known as Varani's Forum Cafe and offers 49 flavours of ice creams and sorbets as well as gluten-free, soya-free, dairy-free and fat-free. The business is enthusiastically run by Ricardo Varani.

John A. Mather & CO.

Bakers and Confectioners.

Telephone No. 404x.

Portland Street & Duke Street
KILMARNOCK.

William Maclachlan was a baker and confectioner with a shop in Titchfield Street. He seems to have taken over the property of Learmont around 1937-38. The baker's shop lasted until about 1969, after which the building was demolished and replaced with a new property.

Gardner was a long established bakery business. In the 1930s William A Gardner was listed as a baker at 27 High Glencairn Street. He lived at 44 Glebe Road. In 1957 the firm was at No. 1 Croft Street, seen here. This became a popular tearoom as well as a shop. The business also had a large bakery in the town. Sadly, like so many small family-owned businesses Gardner's could not compete against the big national franchise companies and the tearoom eventually closed.

The Coffee Club was established in Bank Street in 1959 and quickly earned a good reputation particularly among the young folk of the town. With legendary lemon meringue pies and apple tarts. It is still in Bank Street.

On a straw poll about Kilmarnock shops, one of the favourites was Hector McDonald's camera shop. As a photographic enthusiast, Hector McDonald started his own shop in Kilmarnock in 1920, selling cameras and photographic equipment. For a time the shop was in John Finnie Street. Later it was in Titchfield Street and later still in Bank Street until closing in 2011.

In 1952 Jim Donald of Galston started an electrical business with capital of just £200 and a garden hut for his business premises. Trading as J H Donald, the business became the largest independent electrical trader in the area with shops in five Ayrshire towns, but the firm closed in 2017.

John M Kelso opened his paint and wallpaper shop at 11 Queen Street in 1929, and later moved to No 5. After that No. 11 became the Queen Street Cafe. In 1959 the business moved to Titchfield Steet and the business remained there until 2004, when it became Kelso House to Home and moved to the Forge Industrial Estate off West Langlands Street, at which time it was run by the third generation The move did not pay off and the business closed in 2007.

Kev's Kards in the Foregate is run by Kevin Donaldson. The shop started trading in 1986 and quickly earned a reputation for greeting cards and Scottish souvenirs. It is still in business today.

Hugh Lauder 1841-1916, was a son of John Lauder 1816-97, spirit dealer and Margaret Craig. Hugh set up a department store in Kilmarnock known as the Emporium. His son, Hugh 1877-1935, eventually took this over. It became part of House of Fraser and took on that name in 1975. The shop closed in 1988. The building in this image was destroyed by fire in 1923 and replaced with a more modern one.

Graftons was in King Street. The building was of 1960s construction and after an appeal to the Secretary of State for Scotland, (Willie Ross) it managed to escape the widespread demolition in Kilmarnock town centre in the 1970s and was later used by Manorgrove. It is now the Bank of Scotland.

When visiting Kilmarnock kindly give us a visit

Orders Collected Daily.

Satisfaction Guaranteed.

TELEPHONE 164.

We always carry a large stock of the Finest Groceries & Provisions at the Lowest Market Prices.

Every Customer receives the best personal attention coupled with Civility and Courtesy.

A. M. MILLOY & SON

HIGH-CLASS GROCERS & PROVISION MERCHANTS.

21, Duke Street, :: Kilmarnock.

Quality is the True Test of Cheapness.

Adam Ferguson & Son

FAMILY GROCERS

Tea, Wine, Spirit & Provision Merchants

FAMILIES SUPPLIED WITH GROCERIES AND PROVISIONS AT WHOLESALE RATES

22 and 24, Duke Street

BRANCH SHOP: WOODSTOCK ST. **KILMARNOCK**

Since 1798

The premises at 7, King Street, occupied by Messrs. Rankin & Borland, Chemists, have formed an interesting ancient and unique landmark, as the exterior remains exactly as it was at the end of the 18th Century.

The firm has established a reputation throughout Ayrshire which it has ever been their endeavour to maintain and enhance.

As manufacturers of Aerated Waters they supplied the famous Eglinton Tournament, and the reputation then established has been fully maintained in regard to the quality, flavour and purity of their products.

RANKIN & BORLAND

CHEMISTS

Manufacturers of Aerated Waters

7, King St., Kilmarnock

Established 1798.   Tel. No. 78.

Early 1920s adverts for grocers and chemists in Kilmarnock.

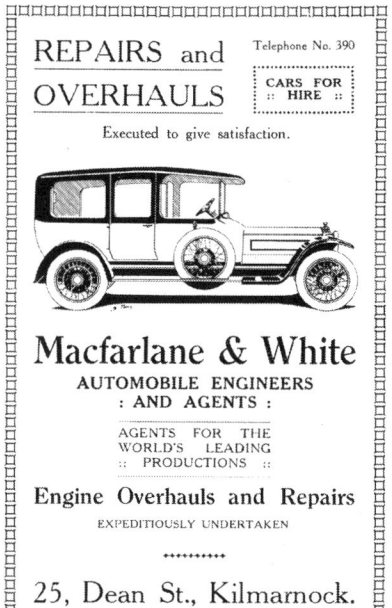

Early 1920s adverts for motor services in Kilmarnock.

Alan Marsh opened his car accessories shop in High Glencairn Street, opposite the Forum Cafe about 1978. He fitted car radios, even to new cars and advertised in the ABC Cinema. In 1987 the business expanded and moved to James Little Street. After Alan retired in 2005 he went into acting.

McCririck was established in 1800 by a gunsmith and was run by the family until 1971. In 1900 the business was in Bank Street and proprietor, William McCririck, lived at Wallacebank in Wellington Street. At that time he was the only gun maker listed in the directory. Up until it closed in 1998, when it was in John Finnie Street, it sold a wide variety of hunting and fishing equipment and services included taxidermy.

EVERYTHING FOR THE GARDEN.

□ □ □

Samsons Limited

Seed Merchants,
Nurserymen and
:: Florists, ::

KILMARNOCK. Established 1759.

Telegraphic Address: "Samsons, Kilmarnock."
Telephone No. 7.

Tam Samson was a seed merchant in Kilmarnock and was a friend of Robert Burns. He even featured in one of the poet's works. The business he founded continued well into the 20th century and eventually became a flower shop.

Donaldson, the fruiterer and florists, was established in 1934 by William Donaldson and after his retirement the business was continued by his nephew, John. In the 1980s they were based in John Finnie Street and described themselves as The Flower People. Next door was a branch of Lauder the Baker, who said they were 'the other flour people'. Lauder the baker, was founded in 1869. The main branch at the Cross had a popular tearoom.

David Lauder was born in 1880, the son of David Lauder the Baker. David, the younger established an ironmongery business in 1901. The shop was at the Cross for many years but due to plans for the redevelopment of the area the business relocated to College Wynd. The firm closed in 2002.

The local firm of John McInnes, ironmonger and tools shop, was established in 1880. In 1930 the business was run by James McInnes and was based in the King's Theatre Building. Today, the shop is in Titchfield Street.

McGougan's was a newsagent at the corner of High Glencairn Street and James Little Street. The shop opened in 1903 and Margaret McGougan took it over in 1904. It remained in the same family for the next 74 years, but changes in the town and the decline of firms like Glenfield & Kennedy meant that business declined to the point where it was no longer viable.

National retailer, Mothercare, opened their Kilmarnock branch in a new building on the corner of King Street and St. Marnock in the 1970s. It soon expanded into a neighbouring unit, but changing shopping patterns meant that it closed in 2014. The building was demolished in 2021 and the site is earmarked for community space.

King Street from St. Marnock Street.

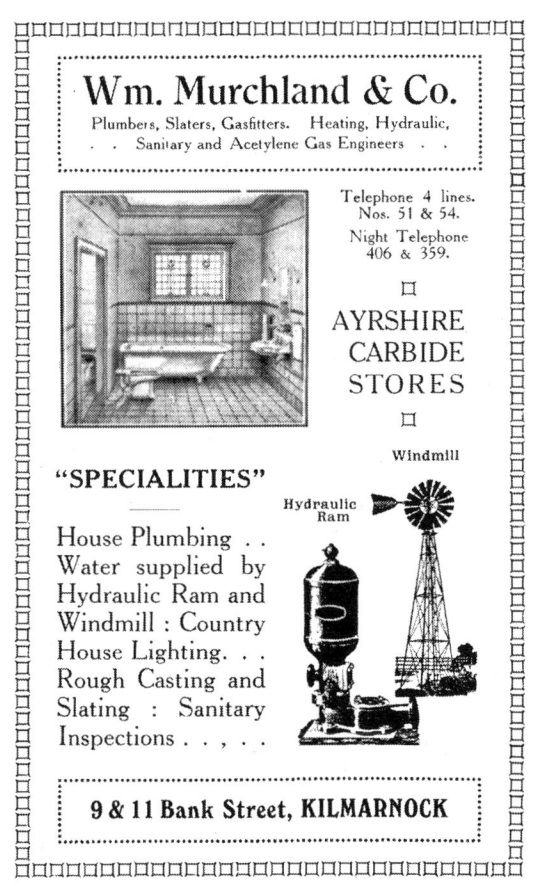

In 1875 William Murchland established his business in Kilmarnock, covering the trades of plumber, slater, tinsmith and gasfitter. He also dealt with a wide variety of goods and services including incandescent gas lighting, mechanical and electrical bells, telephones, heating and ventilation. Like so many other family-owned businesses Murchland is no longer trading, but their legacy lives on. In 1889 William Murchland from Kilmarnock, a plumber, slater, tinsmith and gas fitter, patented the first milking machine. It was a great success and greatly improved the dairy industry, including cheese making.

National retailers Boots and Marks and Spencer both came to King Street in the 1930s. This image shows part of the parade for the 1937 Coronation and clearly work is going on at the Boots site. Marks and Spencer opened their Kilmarnock branch in September, 1936. A 1971 extension to Marks and Spencer shop saw the closure and demolition of the Plaza Cinema and of Mill Lane.

Kilmarnock's favourite pet shop was established in Fore Street. It is listed in the 1957 trades directory as Andrew Muir's shop. It temporarily moved to the corner of Regent Street and Duke Street, then moved to the new Foregate in the 1970s close to the original site seen here.

The Titchfield Street Post Office was opened on October 1st, 1886 with money order and savings bank status. Despite a public protest, it was closed in January, 2004. At that time it was the oldest town sub-office in Kilmarnock.

The family-run firm of Mason Murphy, furniture dealers, was established in Kilmarnock. They have had various locations over the years, including the former George Hotel (later Linds) building in Portland Street,

For many people there was only one place in Kilmarnock to go to get musical instruments and that was RGM. The shop was established in Crookedholm in 1983 by Ian and Loretta Mortimer. They soon outgrew their premises and moved to Kilmarnock, where they became a local fixture. The business closed in 2019.

The A & A Riddick shop sold quality jewellery, gifts and crystal and was run by Anna and Alex Riddick in King Street, Kilmarnock from 1957 until they retired in 1993. The shop continued to trade with their name until about 2002. Soon after that Riddick's opened in Bank Street with the same range of goods. That shop traded until 2014.

Robert Rogerson & Sons was a locally-owned grocery business which specialised in teas, particularly from places like Ceylon (now Sri Lanka). In 1894 they were at 35-37 King Street and later they were at 57-59 King Street. Eventually, they became part of the Coopers chain, which in turn became Fine Fare. Just look at the number of staff in this old picture.

In the early years of the 21st century, T4 Toys was a short-lived toy shop on the corner of Bank Street and College Wynd. It had previously been Beattie's and before that Scotch Corner.

George Tannahill started his business in 1882 and moved his furniture shop to John Finnie Street in 1893. The property may have been custom-built for Tannahill and is in the form of a Glasgow-style shop with tenement accommodation and a vehicle pend. Some of the interior is still in its original style and the shop is hailed as a rare example of its kind. In 1980 the building was given a B status as a listed building and is among other buildings which as a group have an A listing. The building was renovated in 2009-10. It has three storeys, and is of four-bay Glasgow style design with Ballochmyle sandstone; finest example of a period shop front in the conservation area

The long established P & R Torbet, fishing, camping and country-wear shop in John Dickie Street was closed in 2014 due to retirement of the proprietor.

The David Wishart furniture shop in Bank Street was closed in 2000. The company started trading around 1875. However, Wilson's, a new furniture business was opened in the same group of buildings, which were completely refurbished, but keeping the original facade. Today the building is a popular restaurant and bar.

The national retailer, F W Woolworth opened a 3d and 6d shop at the corner of King Street and Market Lane in Kilmarnock in 1925. The photograph on page 23 shows the shop in 1962. The store moved into a large unit in the Burns Shopping Centre in the 1970s. It seems everyone of a certain generation has fond memories of the Pick 'n' Mix or the own-label records, but Woolworths was closed in 2009.